Jesus,
The Ultimate Therapist

HEALING WITHOUT LIMITS

KERRY KERR MCAVOY, PhD

ISBN 13: 978-0-9843205-1-6

Scripture quotations identified (NIV) are taken from the HOLY BIBLE, NEW INTERNATIONAL VERSION®. NIV®. Copyright© 1973, 1978, 1984 by International Bible Society. Used by permission of Zondervan. All rights reserved.

Cover Designed by Lori Vezina
Printed in the United States of America

CONTENT

Introduction

This is the second of a two-part devotional that explores Jesus' desire to have a meaningful, vibrant relationship with us. The first, *Jesus, The Ultimate Therapist: Bringing Hope and Healing*, explores Jesus' competency and sufficiency to bring wholeness and healing to us. Like mental health counselors, he creates a sense of safety and security that allows us to explore our unmet needs and to make our inner selves known. Through this type of relationship with him, we experience personal healing and come to know God better.

This first study used the analogy that Jesus is like the perfect therapist. But this comparison quickly breaks down since our relationship with Jesus exceeds the purposes of all counseling partnerships. He is more than a counselor.

The client-therapist alliance is lop-sided due to the fact that the counselor assumes the role of the expert. As a result, clients trust that the therapist has their best interest at heart. In strong treatment relationships, an appropriate amount of dependence occurs. This is important since support, advice, and healing can only occur under such a situation; but, this also creates vulnerability for patients. State licensing boards and psychological watch groups understand these risks and have instituted legal and ethical mandates to protect consumers. As a result of these protections, mental health clinicians should not treat family members or friends. They are to abstain from developing and acting on romantic feelings toward their clients. Additionally, counselors should be very careful never to use the therapeutic relationship to meet their own emotional needs. These boundaries are in place to protect clients from potential mistreatment and even abuse.

Jesus does not have these restrictions. He never puts his own needs ahead of God's will. He is, by his very nature, love, and, therefore, he perfectly cares, encourages, and cherishes us. Jesus creates the types of relationships with us that go beyond any human example of community or therapeutic alliance. There is no risk with Jesus since he will never exploit, pervert, twist, nor corrupt his relationship with us. He is the *ultimate* therapist, one without boundaries and limits.

This is a nontraditional devotional, in that it uses questions to examine the current condition of your relationship with Jesus. It takes a psychological approach to knowing Christ. How satisfying is your relationship with Jesus? When do you turn to him and why? The intent of this devotional is to increase your understanding of God's desire for you. He yearns for you and is constantly reaching out to draw you closer to him.

You will notice I use questions to explore our belief systems and current spiritual status. As a clinical psychologist, I have learned that real change only happens when there is increased introspection and personal awareness. I cannot change my own attitude or behavior unless I first believe it is an issue. This devotional uses questions to encourage you to stop and examine your belief system. It is not enough to know Jesus; he longs for you to relate personally to him.

I hope you won't just read the material, but will also interact with it. I am going to review some suggestions I made in the first study to aid you in that process. In this book there are six chapters. It is my intention that each chapter be a week-long focus. You will notice each chapter starts with a Key Scripture. This verse sets the tone for the week. You may choose to do some memorization work. This verse might fit that purpose well. At the end of each day's entry there will be questions. They will be there to facilitate your thinking. The questions are just a start. I hope you will go further. That is, do you agree or disagree with the readings? What is new? What is startling? How do the Scripture readings affect you? The questions at the end of each day's reading are to start the process of your investigation of the material.

You may find that you will want to keep a companion journal for note taking. Some ideas I have for the use of a journal are to note other Bible passages or stories that come to your mind as you work through each chapter, to journal your reaction to the study material, or to note songs and events that illuminate where you are with Jesus at that moment.

I have included a meditation exercise for each chapter. As I mentioned before, it is my desire that you should have a personal experience with Jesus. To be in a relationship with someone means there is a "give and take" or mutuality. We need to spend time just "being" with Jesus and "listening" to him. The meditation exercises are designed to help facilitate the listening part of your relationship with him.

Finally, you will find a musical "playlist" of songs at the end of each chapter. I have included them to give you another way to spend time with Jesus. Sometimes a song will illuminate a different thought or idea about God. My playlist is by no means exhaustive or complete. It is just a start. You may have your favorites that capture the spirit of any given chapter. But I hope my song suggestions will add another dimension to your time with Jesus as you work through this study.

Chapter 1

Our Messiah

KEY SCRIPTURE

"Today in the town of David a Savior has been born to you; he is Christ the Lord."

Luke 2:11

What comes to your mind when you hear the word "messiah?" Messiah means "deliverer." Do you need saving? From what?

As a psychologist, people seek my help for interpersonal problems and emotional distress. During the first appointment new clients give me the history of their difficulties. There is a quiet plea on their part for answers. They hope I can make all their pain and complications immediately go away. It often feels like they are looking for a magical solution. Unfortunately and, maybe, fortunately, counseling doesn't work that way. Through the years as a therapist, I have had a few clients leave our first interview feeling frustrated and disappointed that I couldn't instantly "deliver" them from their situations. They were looking for a messiah.

When God finished creating the heavens and earth and everything to populate the earth, he declared his work "very good" (Genesis 1:31). But the human race brought sin into the picture, which changed everything. Now there was an awareness of shame and separation from God. We try to make our own way through life only to fail at it. The story of the prodigal son exemplifies this problem well. This young man took his inheritance from his father and spent it wildly, pursuing pleasures, only to end up in a pig sty eating pods (Luke 15:11 20). Our own way just does not work.

The angels announced long ago that a savior had been born. They proclaimed that he was born to you and me. Their announcement ended with the proclamation that he was Christ the Lord. The Greek word for Christ is actually "Christos," which means "anointed one" or "messiah." The angels were proclaiming Jesus as our Messiah. He came to save us.

OPENING QUESTIONS

What comes to your mind when you think of the word messiah?

Have you ever found yourself aware of your need for a savior? If so, in what circumstances?

What affects your sense of need or lack of need for a messiah?

Meditatio Scripturarum (to contemplate upon the Scripture) is a wonderful form of meditation. For this week, let's focus on the story of the prodigal son found in Luke 15:11–32. Don't read these verses quickly or superficially. Allow them to soak into your heart. Place yourself in the text by being one of the characters in the story. What do you learn as you imagine yourself as this person? What is God saying to you? You might want to change characters, so that one day you are the prodigal son, the next day the father, and so on. How does this change your perspective? What new things do you learn?

PLAYLIST

"Love Enough"

Carried Along Andrew Peterson

"My Deliverer"

The Jesus Record Rich Mullins

"Arise and Be Comforted"

A Grateful People Watermark

"My Savior My God"

Anything Worth Saying Aaron Shust

Our True Condition

KEY READING

The word of the Lord came to me: "Son of man, confront Jerusalem with her detestable practices and say, 'This is what the Sovereign Lord says to Jerusalem: Your ancestry and birth were in the land of the Canaanites; your father was an Amorite and your mother a Hittite. On the day you were born your cord was not cut, nor were you washed with water to make you clean, nor were you rubbed with salt or wrapped in cloths. No one looked on you with pity or had compassion enough to do any of these things for you. Rather, you were thrown out into the open field, for on the day you were born you were despised."

"Later I passed by, and when I looked at you and saw that you were old enough for love, I spread the corner of my garment over you and covered your naked body. I gave you my solemn oath and entered into a covenant with you, declares the Sovereign Lord, and you became mine."

Ezekiel 16:1–5, 8

Have you ever wondered what God sees when he looks at you and me? Does he see our successes and accomplishments? Is he pleased at how intelligent or pretty we are? When humanity was created in the Garden of Eden, God said that his creation was very good. Does he still find us so? These are hard questions. I think that we will never fully grasp our need for a savior if we do not understand our true spiritual and physical condition.

The key reading gives us a glimpse into what God sees when he looks at us. The woman, Jerusalem, was from tribes whom God declared wicked. She was so unwanted and unloved that the most basic care was not given to her; instead, she was thrown into a field to die. God saw her. He saw her nakedness, her desperation, and her hopelessness. He chose her and loved her, not because she was someone special, but because he chose to do so.

A few years ago I had a similar revelation in my life. One day I realized that God did not love me for any quality I had that I thought made me unique. In fact, when I compared myself against an infinite being, I fell pitifully short. I might have been smart, but God's intelligence had no bounds. I might have been able to sing well, but God's voice was perfectly pitched and infinitely creative. My areas of excellence were puny against a perfect, creative, awesome, infinite Creator. I could not offer anything to God that might impress or attract his attention. Jesus' letter to the Laodicean church said that this group of people might have thought they were elite, but, in reality, they were "wretched, pitiful, poor, blind and naked" (Revelation 3:17). The picture was pretty dismal.

If I can find the strength inside myself to face this painful reality of my true condition, then I will become aware of the fact that I am in desperate need of a messiah. I need someone to save me from this helpless place. Jesus longs to be that person. He says, "Here I am! I stand at the door and knock" (Revelation 3:20a). He is right there, waiting to be let in. The question is: will I open the door?

✻ What do you think the key reading or optional readings are saying to you about your spiritual and physical condition?

✻ How does that condition make you feel when you consider Jesus' desire to have fellowship with you (Revelation 3:20a)?

❧ Why do you think God chose to love and save you?

❧ How does this awareness of God's love affect your sense of need for a savior?

PRAYER

Dear Jesus, I am uncomfortable when I realize that I have nothing to offer. This makes me feel very vulnerable. I know that you have always known my pitiful state and loved me anyway. Thank you for such great love that accepts me just as I am.

OPTIONAL READINGS

Exodus 2:23–24

Matthew 5:3–6

Revelation 3:17–18

Jesus, Our Savior

KEY READING

And there were shepherds living out in the fields nearby, keeping watch over their flocks at night. An angel of the Lord appeared to them, and the glory of the Lord shone around them, and they were terrified. But the angel said to them, "Do not be afraid. I bring you good news that will cause great joy for all the people. Today in the town of David a Savior has been born to you; he is the Messiah, the Lord. This will be a sign to you: You will find a baby wrapped in cloths and lying in a manger."

Suddenly a great company of the heavenly host appeared with the angel, praising God and saying,

> *"Glory to God in the highest heaven,*
> *and on earth peace to those on whom his favor rests."*

Luke 2:8–14

Have you ever thought about whom Jesus has come to save? Biblical stories of saviors or deliverers have two major components (see Exodus 2:1–10; 3:2–10; Judges 13:1–24): a specific time with a specific need for help, and God's surprising, miraculous intervention. Where are those circumstances transpiring today? Many of the special conditions like those found in the mentioned verses are not occurring. Not all of us are Jewish. Generally, we are not slaves or prisoners. If the authors of the Old Testament stories are saying the conditions of needing a savior are gone, then we are in trouble. Are we without hope and on our own? Or could these stories of old be saying more than God helped a specific group of people during a particular period of time?

Let's look closer at the story in which God chose Abram to father a nation. God told Abram that "all the peoples on earth will be blessed through you" (Genesis 12:3b). Luke tells us that Jesus is the fulfillment of this promise. He records that the angel of the Lord told the shepherds Jesus' birth was "good news of great joy that will be for *all the people*" (Luke 2:10, author's emphasis). This was not just for a few of us, the lucky ones by birth or blood. This news was for all of us. These stories of "deliverers" were not just to comfort a few of us, but to encourage all of us. We have a hope, and his name is Jesus.

❦ When you read of God making a nation from Abram, do you feel a sense of connectedness and hope? Why or why not?

❦ What do you think God was doing by choosing Abram to bless all of us?

❦ What does it mean to you that Jesus is to bring great joy to all of us?

PRAYER

Dear Jesus, thank you for being the fulfillment of the promise made to Abram so long ago. You have come to bring us hope and great joy. Let that hope and joy grow in my heart today.

OPTIONAL READINGS

Genesis 17:15–17, 19; 21:1–7

Jesus and Wrong Expectations

KEY READING

When Jesus came to the region of Caesarea Philippi, he asked his disciples, "Who do people say the Son of Man is?"

They replied, "Some say John the Baptist; others say Elijah; and still others, Jeremiah or one of the prophets."

"But what about you?" he asked. "Who do you say I am?"

Simon Peter answered, "You are the Messiah, the Son of the living God."

Jesus replied, "Blessed are you, Simon son of Jonah, for this was not revealed to you by flesh and blood, but by my Father in heaven. And I tell you that you are Peter, and on this rock I will build my church, and the gates of Hades will not overcome it. I will give you the keys of the kingdom of heaven; whatever you bind on earth will be bound in heaven, and whatever you loose on earth will be loosed in heaven." Then he ordered his disciples not to tell anyone that he was the Messiah.

Matthew 16:13–20

When reading the account of Jesus as recorded in the four Gospels, have you ever noticed the confusion around Jesus' identity and purpose? Even John the Baptist, the forerunner of Jesus' ministry, had doubts. Herod was threatened by Jesus, so the king slaughtered all the boys less than two years of age in Bethlehem. Later, Pharisees were angered and plotted to kill Jesus. Even his own disciples struggled with his purpose: one betrayed him, one denied him, and one doubted him.

Why such confusion and anger? Why not excitement and anticipation? Sure, there were many folks who sought Jesus, but when it got tough, even his disciples abandoned him. Again, why did they misunderstand? I believe it was because of wrong expectations about the messiah's purpose. The Jewish people were under the Roman Empire's heavy control. They might have been hoping for someone to lead them out from under that government. Moses led the Israelites out of Egyptian control. They had been delivered from the Assyrians, Babylonians, and Philistines; so, why not the Romans?

The people of Jesus' time did not understand that his purposes were greater than their hopes and plans. How many times do we do the same thing? We develop doubts, and our faith and trust become particularly tested when life circumstances are unexpectedly hard or going wrong. It is easy to follow Jesus when all is going well, but do we still believe that his plans are best when we are sick or we've lost our job or when a family member is dying? Those are the times when the question Jesus poses to his disciples becomes a real test: "Who do you say that I am?" Is Jesus still our Messiah then? He longs to be.

❊ What situations have threatened your confidence in Jesus as your Messiah?

❊ Why do those situations threaten your trust?

❊ What have you done to get through such times with your faith intact?

❊ How do you think Jesus wants to meet you in those times?

PRAYER

Dear Jesus, you long to be my savior and messiah. You have come to save me. Forgive me when my expectations do not match up with your plans. Strengthen my trust in you so that I can have greater faith when life is hard or difficult.

OPTIONAL READINGS

Matthew 2:1–13; 26:57–67

Luke 7:18–27

Jesus, the Promised Messiah

KEY READING

The Spirit of the Sovereign Lord is on me,
because the Lord has anointed me
to proclaim good news to the poor.
He has sent me to bind up the brokenhearted,
to proclaim freedom for the captives
and release from darkness for the prisoners,
to proclaim the year of the Lord's favor
and the day of vengeance of our God,
to comfort all who mourn,
and provide for those who grieve in Zion—
to bestow on them a crown of beauty
instead of ashes,
the oil of joy
instead of mourning,
and a garment of praise
instead of a spirit of despair.
They will be called oaks of righteousness,
a planting of the Lord
for the display of his splendor.

Isaiah 61:1–3

Don't you get excited when you read through the descriptions of the Messiah found in today's readings? Jesus has come to usher in God's kingdom that promises peace, justice, freedom, healing, and restoration. He has come to restore what was lost when sin entered the world. The confusion surrounding him is understandable, since much of this work needs to be done in the hearts of each person. Remember Adam and Eve's first response to their new condition of sin? They suddenly became aware of their nakedness and hid. Shame and self-consciousness entered the world. The human race became preoccupied with itself, instead of God. This led to rapidly increasing wickedness: from Cain killing Abel to such unfettered wickedness that God flooded the whole earth and started over with Noah.

Jesus now provides a new way. He comes to bring true change and real hope. He isn't about just changing our current socioeconomic condition or even the current world governments. He is doing something much more profound. He comes to bring healing to our sin-filled, broken heart. Jesus puts "an undivided heart and. . . a new spirit" in us (Ezekiel 11:19). He ushers in God's will where each of us has substituted our own will. Jesus comes to save us, and, in that act, the whole world is changed. Paul says it this way: "Therefore, if anyone is in Christ, he is a new creation; the old has gone, the new has come! All this is from God, who reconciled us to himself through Christ and gave us the ministry of reconciliation: that God was reconciling the world to himself in Christ, not counting men's sins against them" (2 Corinthians 5:17–19a). What must you do to be saved and changed like that? Just call out to Jesus and he will save you (Romans 10:10–13).

❧ If you have trusted Jesus to save you, describe the change this has brought to your life since you are a "new creation in Christ."

❧ How are you seeing the kingdom of God being ushered in through your life as you trust in Christ?

PRAYER

Dear Jesus, thank you for being my Messiah. Thank you for saving me and for giving me an undivided heart and a new spirit. Let me be a part of your ministry of reconciliation in my corner of the world.

OPTIONAL READINGS

Isaiah 11:1–5; 53:1–12

Luke 7:18–21

Concluding Thoughts

A friend recently called me. Her husband had lost his job and subsequently their health insurance. She was dealing with several health issues. She told me she felt out of control and scared. Due to all the uncertainty in her life, she started to have regular episodes of panic attacks. She wanted to know how to go about looking for a good counselor.

From time to time, we may find ourselves needing a professional opinion. Some people feel surprised and even embarrassed by their need for counseling. It can feel weak to want someone's help with difficult and complicated life circumstances. However, this neediness isn't weakness, it is strength. Research has found that the most resilient individuals appropriately use outside intervention.

Likewise, we need a savior. We need someone to rescue us not only from our troubling situations, but also from our spiritual condition of sinfulness. Jesus has come to be that person to us. Right now he is waiting to be invited into all of our circumstances. The question remains whether or not we will recognize our need for Jesus' intervention.

Chapter 2
The Lamb of God

KEY SCRIPTURE

"Look, the Lamb of God, who takes away the sin of the world!"

John 1:29

As a therapist, I dislike the times when my personal life interferes with and affects my clinical work. Usually such hindrances are outside of my control, such as an illness, pregnancy, or a death in the family. This conflict has occurred in my life and practice during my three pregnancies. Each time I found my physical and emotional resources below normal. I was easily fatigued and potentially distractible. I worried about how this intrusion of my personal life would affect my clients' treatment experiences.

A particular instance stands out in my mind. During one of my pregnancies, I had a struggling client who needed extra support. She called me a few times due to an emotional crisis during late night hours, interrupting my sleep. It worried me that I might not have enough inner resources to meet her particular needs. I didn't want to resent her intrusions. After all, she needed my help and had my permission to call. My limitations were my responsibilities. It was very important that I remain supportive and responsive to her, but I knew I was only human.

Jesus does not have these same limitations. He is inexhaustible. His intercession is constant. His patience is never-ending. Jesus' availability has no end. He did not even withhold his own life to save you and me. He has come to be our Lamb.

What does this mean? In these enlightened modern times do we still need a sacrificial lamb like Old Testament worshippers? What is the function of the sacrifice?

Humanity's troubles started at the beginning of time with Adam and Eve's expulsion from the Garden of Eden. This was a literal and symbolic representation of the loss of intimacy that God had created for them. They also brought on themselves the penalty of death: the death of their relationship with God (or spiritual death) and the physical death of their living bodies. The penalty did not stop there. All of creation would live with the consequences of unleashed sinfulness. Paul records that "the creation was subjected to frustration, not by its own choice, but by the will of the one who subjected it, in hope that the creation itself will be liberated from its bondage to decay and brought into the glorious freedom of the children of God" (Romans 8:20–21). All of creation was brought down by Adam and Eve's disobedience.

This problem does not end with Adam and Eve. Over and again this pattern occurred. God offered us his best, even himself. But the human race settled instead for itself, which, in the end, was nothing but emptiness.

Why do we persist in doing this? Despite how disturbing this question is, the more perplexing one is why God would send us his son, Jesus, and offer him as our once-and-for-all-sacrifice? I would think after thousands of years of trying to save us, God would throw up his hands in exasperation and frustration. I would expect he would give us what we deserve: death. But God does the most surprising thing. He provides a way perfectly and completely to pay for our separation and sin. God's love has no bounds, and he withholds nothing; not even his son to save us from ourselves. God has sacrificed Jesus, and Jesus, our Lamb, willingly went.

How do patterns of sin show up in your life?

How does this repeated pattern of sin make you feel?

What comes to your mind when you think of Jesus as the Lamb?

MEDITATION EXERCISE

Breath prayer is a short, simple prayer that can be said in one breath. For the purpose of this chapter, I suggest you use a sentence that focuses on Jesus as the Lamb of God, such as "The Lamb of God takes away my sins." This is a modification of the Key Scripture for this week. Find a quiet place where you can be alone and take five to fifteen minutes to focus on your breath prayer. This prayer is to be spoken silently within yourself in a relaxed manner. As you repeat it, listen to how God uses this prayer to speak to you. What is your reaction to the words? How are you responding to God? After several minutes of repeating the breath prayer, reflect on what you are hearing from God. You may want to write out these reflections in a journal.

PLAYLIST

"Via Dolorosa"

Love Is On The Move Leeland

"Revelation Song"

Fearless Phillips, Craig & Dean

"In Amazing Grace Land"

So Far: The Best of Susan Ashton, Vol. 1 Susan Ashton

"Still the Cross"

Still The Cross FFH

Isaac and Jesus, Beloved Sons

KEY READING

When they reached the place God had told him about, Abraham built an altar there and arranged the wood on it. He bound his son Isaac and laid him on the altar, on top of the wood. Then he reached out his hand and took the knife to slay his son. But the angel of the Lord called out to him from heaven, "Abraham! Abraham!"

"Here I am," he replied.

"Do not lay a hand on the boy," he said. "Do not do anything to him. Now I know that you fear God, because you have not withheld from me your son, your only son."

Genesis 22:9–12

The story of Abraham and Isaac is a fascinating one. Abraham waited years to have a child. How precious and miraculous was Isaac's birth. I wonder what went through Abraham's mind as he walked to Mount Moriah. Would God really require him to give up his much loved and longed for son? Why would God give miraculously only to take his gift away? Would Abraham obey? I can hardly put myself in Abraham's position. I have three sons, yet I would rather die than take the life of one of my children.

We have the benefit of the lens of time to understand this story. We see the theme of testing Abraham's devotion to God, but the story symbolizes much more. This is foreshadowing of Jesus' death. Just as Abraham was asked to make a journey of sacrifice, God, too, would make a similar journey with his own precious son, Jesus. This second time there would be no substitute for the child when the moment of sacrifice came. Instead,

God would offer up his one and only son as a sacrifice for the whole world. God would not pull back from such a horrible loss. What great love God has for you and me to give his one and only son to save us all.

* What stands out as different or new when you compare Abraham and Isaac's story with Jesus' sacrifice?

* How does it impact you to think of God as a father giving up his much loved son?

* When Jesus told the crowd that God would give his one and only son, do you think Jesus understood the "giving" would mean a sacrificial type of giving involving his own life?

* How does this change the picture to think that Jesus knowingly walked toward the cross to redeem you?

PRAYER

Dear God, thank you for loving me enough to give your one and only son to save me from my sins. I don't deserve this sacrifice. Help me let the awareness of your deep love sink into the center of my being.

OPTIONAL READINGS

John 3:16

Jesus, the Passover Lamb

KEY READING

"On that same night I will pass through Egypt and strike down every firstborn of both people and animals, and I will bring judgment on all the gods of Egypt. I am the Lord. The blood will be a sign for you on the houses where you are, and when I see the blood, I will pass over you. No destructive plague will touch you when I strike Egypt."

Exodus 12:12–13

God ordered Moses to go to Pharaoh ten times and demand the Israelites be set free to worship their God. Despite nine horrific plagues, Pharaoh's heart was unmoved. God was about to demonstrate his authority in the tenth plague. Moses warned Pharaoh that there would be loud wailing throughout Egypt—"worse than there has ever been or ever will be again" (Exodus 11:6). The Angel of Death was about to pass over every household and strike the firstborn dead of every family. God made a distinction between Egyptians and Israelites. The Israelites were to sacrifice a lamb and wipe its blood on the sides and the top of the door frames. After doing everything God commanded, the people would wait while the Angel of Death passed over the area. Everyone was left alive in the Israelites' households, while all the firstborns in the Egyptians' homes died.

This miracle is not just a reminder of God's faithfulness thousands of years ago. The miracle continues today. All of us are like the firstborn in the Egyptians' households. We are under a sentence of death. But when you or I accept Jesus as our savior, as our personal Passover Lamb, then the penalty of death that hangs over our head is taken away. We are forgiven and our sentence of death is absolved. The author of Hebrews tells us that Jesus knowingly offered himself as the Passover Lamb. "Let us fix our eyes on Jesus, the author and perfecter of our faith, who for the joy set before him endured the cross" (Hebrews 12:2). You and I are that joy. Jesus saw the act of saving us as one he was willing to endure.

How does it change your thinking to see Jesus as your Passover Lamb?

Just as the Israelites obediently wiped blood on the doorpost of their homes, what act of faith do you follow to demonstrate your trust in God?

PRAYER

Dear Jesus, thank you for being my Passover Lamb. I do not deserve such a sacrifice. To think that you considered it a joy to endure the cross for me is overwhelming. Let the truth of your love fill my heart.

OPTIONAL READINGS

1 Corinthians 5:7–8

1 Peter 1:18–21

Jesus and the System of Offerings

KEY READING

First he said, "Sacrifices and offerings, burnt offerings and sin offerings you did not desire, nor were you pleased with them"—though they were offered in accordance with the law. Then he said, "Here I am, I have come to do your will." He sets aside the first to establish the second. And by that will, we have been made holy through the sacrifice of the body of Jesus Christ once for all.

Hebrews 10:8–10

A holy God and unholy human race; how can this impossible gap be crossed? God longs for a relational connection with each man and woman but cannot contaminate himself with our sinfulness. God is love and holiness and truth and righteousness. Humanity has chosen selfishness, bitterness, revenge, self-deception, and self-righteousness. Like oil and water the two cannot blend and mingle.

Once Adam and Eve sinned, humanity's relationship with God was affected. So, God set in place a system of sacrifices and offerings to cleanse his people from their sins. This cleansing was temporary, requiring annual offerings to cover the people's sins. Hebrews tells us that "day after day every priest stands and performs his religious duties; again and again he offers the same sacrifices, which can never take away sins" (Hebrews 10:11).

Jesus came and offered a better way. He became the "once and for all" sacrifice. He is the perfect lamb that, if accepted, covers our sins permanently. We are freed from our sinful hearts; we are freed from the need for the regular offerings and sacrifices; we are freed once again to relate to a holy God.

❦ How have your seen your sinful nature show up?

❦ How have you tried to be a good person outside the help of God? How effective have your efforts been?

❦ What does it feel like to know that you are set free from your sinfulness by your acceptance of Jesus' sacrifice?

❦ How does this forgiveness and freedom change things for you?

PRAYER

Thank you, Jesus, for being the perfect sacrifice that sets me free from my sinful ways and my wayward heart. If there is any continuing false guilt or a sense of doubt that I am not completely forgiven, please break that falsehood in my heart. I want to experience relief from any lingering guilt or shame.

OPTIONAL READINGS

Exodus 20

Leviticus 19:2

Jesus the Spotless, Worthy Lamb

KEY READING

But we have this treasure in jars of clay to show that this all-surpassing power is from God and not from us. We are hard pressed on every side, but not crushed; perplexed, but not in despair; persecuted, but not abandoned; struck down, but not destroyed. We always carry around in our body the death of Jesus, so that the life of Jesus may also be revealed in our body. For we who are alive are always being given over to death for Jesus' sake, so that his life may also be revealed in our mortal body.

Therefore we do not lose heart. Though outwardly we are wasting away, yet inwardly we are being renewed day by day. For our light and momentary troubles are achieving for us an eternal glory that far outweighs them all. So we fix our eyes not on what is seen, but on what is unseen, since what is seen is temporary, but what is unseen is eternal.

2 Corinthians 4:7–11, 16–18

Several years ago, I was sitting across from a female client who was sharing her story of childhood abuse. It was painful to listen to, but I have heard many such stories. As I listened I recalled a radio interview with holocaust survivor, Corrie ten Boom, who shared that she believed God was creating a beautiful tapestry out of the stories of our lives.[1] I prayed during that appointment and asked God what picture he was creating with our life stories. Suddenly, I had a vision. In my mind's eye I saw two hands holding an unrolled tapestry. As the face of the canvas was almost visible, the picture was blacked out. I heard in my head a clear voice announcing that the picture was of "The Lamb."

As I have pondered this vision, I've discovered that the book of Revelation's main reference to Jesus is as "The Lamb." This book of the

Bible has thirty-one references to Jesus, the Lamb. They include the Slain Lamb, the Worthy Lamb, the Lamb's throne, the Lamb's bride, the Lamb's wedding, and the Lamb's book of life. There is an almost exclusive focus of the personhood of Jesus as the Lamb.

Could this focus emphasize Jesus' difference? He is humble and completely submitted to the will of his Father. He follows through with being the substituted sacrifice, even to the point of being crucified on the cross. He saves the world by his obedience to the cross. It is by his slain body and spilt blood that our debt or wages of sin are paid. He freely gives this. He does it for "the joy set before him" (Hebrews 2:12).

The continued use of the name "Lamb" for Jesus could also be to draw attention to the completion or permanence of the payment or "atonement." He is the sacrificial lamb "once and for all." The original judgment by God in the Garden of Eden that Adam and Eve "would surely die" (Genesis 2:17) has been satisfied by Jesus' death. Never again will there need to be another sacrifice. The debt is paid.

I suspect there is another reason for Revelation's emphasis of Jesus as the Lamb of God. It is something I learned from that vision years ago. I believe that all of our life stories, including our triumphs, tragedies, and pain, are being redeemed by Jesus. These painful occurrences can become opportunities for Jesus to demonstrate his presence and power in our lives. It is recorded in 2 Corinthians that "though outwardly we are wasting away, yet inwardly we are being renewed day by day" (2 Corinthians 4:16). Jesus, the Lamb of God, has delivered every minute of our lives. Nothing we suffer will be wasted; instead, it will be used to bring glory to God (2 Corinthians 4:17–18). And one day, all of death and sin will come to an end because of his great sacrifice.

How do you explain to others why good people suffer?

How have you seen Jesus use your life story to manifest his power and victory over sin?

What other thoughts do you have about why the author of Revelation continually referred to Jesus as the Lamb?

PRAYER

Dear Jesus, thank you for being the worthy Lamb of God. Because of you, I can be set free from sin and have a relationship with you. Thank you for using all of my life experiences to demonstrate your victory over sin. Remind me to focus on eternity when I get discouraged.

OPTIONAL READINGS

Romans 8:18, 28–38

Concluding Thoughts

Our psychological and spiritual needs are great. We long to be worthy of another's attention. We desire to be understood and cherished. Finally, we need to be rescued from our selfish and sinful condition. Counselors can meet some of these needs, some of the time, but on a limited scale. Therapists cannot be there for every crisis nor can they perfectly understand every situation, despite best efforts. They cannot truly know the heart of another, nor can they be constantly available, however Jesus can. He withholds nothing to love and restore us. He is our perfect, worthy Lamb.

Chapter 3

Our Kinsman-Redeemer

KEY SCRIPTURE

"But when the time had fully come, God sent his Son, born of a woman, born under the law, to redeem those under law, that we might receive the full rights of sons."

Galatians 4:4–5

Occasionally I receive a telephone call from close friends who are looking for a counselor. I always refer them to another mental health clinician. My friends are disappointed that I can't be their therapist.

Ethical guidelines prohibit therapists from treating family members, friends and close acquaintances. This limitation makes sense. It would hard to be objective about a personal situation. A therapist would be drawn to protect his or her interest. Counselors are supposed to be emotionally uninvolved. Once a personal relationship is present, this distance is lost.

Scripture identifies Jesus as our family, yet he does not need to maintain these same boundaries. He can be emotionally involved, yet restore and heal us.

To better understand this familial role, it is important to appreciate what kinsman–redeemer meant during biblical times. In Jesus' day, a Hebrew woman had few rights. Her legal rights came to her by way of her father, later her husband, and finally her son. She would live in her father's house until married. After marriage her husband would assume responsibility for her needs.

Women having male children were particularly blessed since a son's role was critical to the family's future. The son would have many obligations to his parents. The fifth commandment of honoring one's parents had ramifications. The Talmud is full of specific commands regarding the responsibilities a son had to his parents, including financial and physical needs. When the father died, the son was the sole heir with the mandate to provide for his minor sisters and his widowed mother.

Since so much has changed in Western cultures, including this type of family structure, do we still need a kinsman-redeemer? What does it mean when Jesus says that "whoever does the will of my Father in heaven is my brother and sister and mother" (Matthew 12:50)? I think there is much to this role of kinsman-redeemer that is important, yet not fully understood by our present culture. I suspect our need for Jesus' redemptive work is very great. Let's explore what it means for us that Jesus became our kinsman-redeemer. Maybe we will be stirred and excited as Zechariah when he prophesied, "Praise be to the Lord, the God of Israel, because he has come and has redeemed his people" (Luke 1:68).

OPENING QUESTIONS

What role does family play in your life?

What do you know about the function of kinsman-redeemer?

MEDITATION EXERCISE

Let's practice the meditation exercise called "palms down, palms up." Place your palms in your lap in an upright position as if to receive something. Identify the troubling areas in your life. Imagine these things are resting in the palms of your hands. Now turn your palms downward. Imagine yourself letting them fall at the feet of Jesus and pray a releasing prayer, such as "I release my anxiety about my job." After taking some time to surrender these areas of concern, turn your palms upward. This time receive God's comfort. For example, you might pray "Lord, I receive your encouragement and peace as I face these issues at work." Spend several minutes in silence with your heart listening to what else God might be saying to you.

PLAYLIST

"Spoken For"

Spoken For MercyMe

"You Deliver Me"

You Deliver Me Selah

"I Will Sing of My Redeemer"

This Bright Hour Fernando Ortega

The Role of the Family

KEY READING

In the days when the judges ruled, there was a famine in the land. So a man from Bethlehem in Judah, together with his wife and two sons, went to live for a while in the country of Moab. The man's name was Elimelek, his wife's name was Naomi, and the names of his two sons were Mahlon and Kilion. They were Ephrathites from Bethlehem, Judah. And they went to Moab and lived there.

Now Elimelek, Naomi's husband, died, and she was left with her two sons. The married Moabite women, one named Orpah and the other Ruth. After they had *lived there about ten years, both Mahlon and Kilion also died, and Naomi was left without her two sons and her husband.*

Then Naomi said to her two daughters-in-law, "Go back, each of you, to your mother's home. May the Lord show you kindness, as you have shown kindness to your dead husbands and to me. May the Lord grant that each of you will find rest in the home of another husband."

Ruth 1:1–5, 8–9

During Jesus' day the definition of family consisted not only of parents and children, but it also included grandparents, grandchildren and servants. Childbirth was seen as an important part of a woman's life (1 Timothy 2:15) and children were a blessing from the Lord (Psalm 127:3). Of all the family members, the most vulnerable were the children and women. As a result, the law recognized this vulnerability by providing extra security. For example, Alfred Edersheim, in his book *Sketches of Jewish Social Life*, noted there were four obligations a wife was required to observe toward her husband, whereas he was bound by ten obligations to his wife. These obligations included requirements to take care of her medical needs to give her a respectable funeral, to provide her a place in his home, to support financially her daughters, and to give an inheritance to her sons.

Without a grown son, widowhood was devastating. A widow could not inherit from her husband. Without close kin to marry, she was without financial support. Judah left Tamar in a terrible position (Genesis 38). She had no choice but to become an unwanted financial burden to her family. She was without position or standing. Naomi found herself in a similar position. For sustenance, she was left to depend on Ruth gleaning food from grain fields being harvested. So desperate was a widow or orphan's plight that James considered looking after them as part of a faultless walk with God (James 1:27).

In Western civilization women do not find themselves as dependent on a relationship with a male relative (father, husband, or son) for their futures. Orphaned children, however, are not as fortunate. Upon whom or what do you depend? What gives you standing or security? Your retirement fund? Your marriage? Your job? Being a widow or an orphan in those times was a picture of abject powerlessness. They were without influence or means. Just because family connections are not the same as they were in Jesus' day does not lessen your risk. You can still find yourself vulnerable and powerless, just in a different manner.

❦ How do such desperate positions occur today?

❦ Have you ever found yourself in a position of powerlessness?

🦎 Who/what did you count on for help in that situation?

🦎 Do you think being aware of one's vulnerability is helpful or hurtful? Why?

PRAYER

Dear Jesus, thank you for helping me when I find myself in trouble. You see me, and you see my condition. Please make me more aware of you and your concern for my situation. Please open my eyes to see others who are in need of help.

OPTIONAL READINGS

Genesis 38

Luke 7:11–14

The Role of the Kinsman-Redeemer

KEY READING

Then Boaz announced to the elders and all the people, "Today you are witnesses that I have bought from Naomi all the property of Elimelek, Kilion and Mahlon. I have also acquired Ruth the Moabite, Mahlon's widow, as my wife, in order to maintain the name of the dead with his property, so that his name will not disappear from among his family or from his hometown. Today you are witnesses!"

So Boaz took Ruth and she became his wife. When he made love to her, the Lord enabled her to conceive, and she gave birth to a son. The women said to Naomi: "Praise be to the Lord, who this day has not left you without a guardian-redeemer. May he become famous throughout Israel! He will renew your life and sustain you in your old age. For your daughter-in-law, who loves you and who is better to you than seven sons, has given him birth."

Ruth 4:9–10. 13 –15

A kinsman-redeemer. What exactly is this role? The need for restoration was common among these people. The Old Testament described four conditions which required a redeemer.

- If a woman's husband died and she was without a son, she was to be married to one of her husband's brothers. The first child born to this union would carry on the name of her first husband so that his line and name could be continued (Genesis 38:8; Ruth 3–4).

- If a man became poor and had to sell off his land, his nearest relative could buy back the land to return it to its original owner, thus protecting the man's livelihood (Leviticus 25:25).

- If a man became poor and sold himself or his family into slavery, his nearest relative could buy him or his family out of slavery and restore his/their freedom (Leviticus 25:47).

- If a man was murdered, his nearest relative could act as an avenger and pursue the killer (Deuteronomy 19:1–3; Numbers 35:26).

All of these described dire conditions in which one finds himself or herself out of control and without power. Through an act of compassion and intervention, a kinsman-redeemer could change all of that. In fact, the name kinsman-redeemer is the Hebrew word "goel," which means to "buy back" or "to redeem."

Just as there are specific conditions with the need for redemption, there are certain requirements that a redeemer must meet. We see these requirements alluded to in Ruth's story. A kinsman-redeemer must be related. Boaz was a close relative to Ruth's in-laws. He must also have the means by which to redeem. Boaz was a financially successful man who was able to provide for Naomi and Ruth. There must be a willingness on the part of the redeemer to intercede. There was a closer relative to Naomi's family, but he was not interested when he learned that redemption meant acquiring the dead man's widow (see Ruth 4:2–6), whereas Boaz was willing to take on this responsibility. Finally, a kinsman-redeemer needs to follow through and complete the redemptive act. Boaz announced to the elders and people, in Ruth 4:9–10, that he would buy the property of Naomi's husband and sons and marry Ruth.

⯌ What is your reaction to the role of kinsman-redeemer?

🌿 Do we have a modern day version of kinsman-redeemer?

🌿 Have you ever had someone redeem something for you? What was that like? How did it make you feel?

PRAYER

Dear Jesus, thank you for this beautiful concept of kinsman-redeemer. Make this role very personal to me. Let me see more clearly what aspects of myself and my life need to be redeemed.

OPTIONAL READINGS

Deuteronomy 19:1–3, 25:5

Numbers 35:12–34

Leviticus 25: 25, & 47–49

Ruth 3:1–4

Our Need for a Kinsman-Redeemer

KEY READING

"Later I passed by, and when I looked at you and saw that you were old enough for love, I spread the corner of my garment over you and covered your naked body. I gave you my solemn oath and entered into a covenant with you, declares the Sovereign Lord, and you became mine."

Ezekiel 16:

What does this concept of kinsman-redeemer have to do with you and me? I have seen clients whose outward life looks well put together but their inward life is full of insecurity and fear. I've listened to many stories of unfair treatment and abuse. I am able to help most of these individuals, but it makes me aware of how fortunate we are to have Jesus as our Kinsman-Redeemer.

We live in a culture that focuses on the nuclear family and the "self made man." We have a justice system to deal with crimes. We do not live in a society that allows for slavery in order to pay off debts. Often widows do not live in a state of poverty but are able to acquire skills and work. Do we still need a kinsman-redeemer?

Revelation 3:17 suggests that we do. This is Jesus' letter to the church of Laodicea, which apparently was a fairly wealthy church. "You say, am rich; I have acquired wealth, and do not need a thing." (Doesn't that sound like a rephrasing of my starting paragraph?) Then the writer goes on to say, "But you do not realize that you are wretched, pitiful, poor blind and naked." Ouch. This same theme shows up in Ezekiel 16 with the description of the girl called "Jerusalem." She was unwanted, unloved and naked. She was tossed out into the fields to be eaten by animals to die from exposure. The allegory is drawing a connection between her plight and ours. We are Jerusalem.

The Beatitudes start out similarly. Jesus uses words like "poor in spirit," "mourning," and "hunger" to describe our condition. The need for a kinsman-redeemer first starts with the recognition that one is in a desperate state of utter helplessness and spiritual poverty. We cannot receive help unless we start with our recognition of this reality.

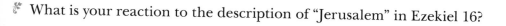 What is your reaction to the description of "Jerusalem" in Ezekiel 16?

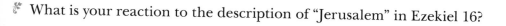 What gets in the way of your awareness of your need for a kinsman-redeemer?

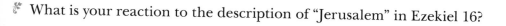 How have you become aware of your desperate state of need?

PRAYER

Dear Jesus, looking at my spiritual condition outside of you is very painful. I often avoid facing my need for you. Forgive me for my self-reliance. Help me to depend on you and to see you as my Kinsman-Redeemer.

OPTIONAL READINGS

Matthew 5:1–6

Revelation 3:17

Jesus, Our Willing Kinsman-Redeemer

KEY READING

The Spirit you received does not make you slaves, so that you live in fear again;
rather, the Spirit you received brought about your adoption to sonship. And by
him we cry, "Abba, Father." The Spirit himself testifies with our spirit that we
are God's children. Now if we are children, then we are heirs—heirs of God and
co-heirs with Christ, if indeed we share in his sufferings in order that we may
also share in his glory.

Romans 8:15–17

During my youth, I sang at church a popular Christian song that spoke about being a part of God's family. This is still true. When we trust in Jesus, we become a member of God's family (Matthew 12:48–50). This means we can ask Jesus to be our Kinsman-Redeemer. Remember that one of the requirements of kinsman-redeemer was that he must be a close relative. If we are family, then Jesus becomes our close relative, thus he can be our Kinsman-Redeemer.

There are three other requirements to be met in order for Jesus to be our Kinsman-Redeemer. He must have the means, the willingness, and the follow through to redeem you and me. Paul, in his letter to the Philippians, addresses these conditions in a very clear manner. He says, "Who [referring to Jesus], being in very nature of God, did not consider equality with God something to be grasped, but made himself nothing, taking the very nature of a servant, being made in human likeness. And being found in appearance as a man, he humbled himself and became obedient to death—even death on a cross!" (2:6–8).

Jesus has the means: he is the very nature of God. He is willing: he humbled himself and became obedient. And Jesus completed the act: he was obedient to death, thus paying for our sins. Jesus is our Kinsman Redeemer. Because of him, we are set free or "redeemed" from our slavery to sin, our wretched needy spiritual condition, and our utterly helpless state. I like the way Paul puts it in Titus 2:14: "[Jesus] gave himself for us to redeem us from all wickedness and to purify for himself a people that are his very own, eager to do what is good."

❦ What does it feel like to realize Jesus is your "brother?"

❦ What one thing will change in your life as you continue to accept Jesus' "redemption?"

PRAYER

Dear Jesus, thank you for being my Kinsman-Redeemer. I am overwhelmed by your willingness to assume this role for me. Thank you for redeeming me, for buying me back from my slavery to sin.

OPTIONAL READINGS

Matthew 12:48–50

John 10:17–18

Philippians 2:6–8

Concluding Thoughts

Just as women in Jesus' day were without legal rights, so are we spiritually dependent. Jesus wants to restore our situation. If we accept him as our savior, we become part of his family. With this association come many privileges, including Jesus becoming our Kinsman-Redeemer. He has come to redeem us or buy us back from our sinful condition. There is a condition to this help. Just as I cannot counsel someone who does not believe he or she requires any mental health services, Jesus cannot redeem us if we don't recognize our need for his intervention.

Chapter 4

Our Friend

"You are my friends if you do what I command."

John 15:14

Friendship with Jesus—what an amazing concept! What comes to your mind when you think of the word "friend?" Have you had good experiences? Are you one of those people who seems to be surrounded by friends? Or are you more of a loner, someone who finds making friends hard. Or maybe you just prefer your own company.

Friendship is a special type of relationship. It brings a sense of camaraderie to our lives and creates a history of shared experiences for us. Psychologists know that those of us who have rich social connections are often healthier. We are more resistant to illnesses and have improved psychological resilience under stressful conditions.

Jesus does a surprising thing. He announces to his disciples that if they prove obedient to his will, they will be his friends. I wonder what went through their minds when they heard his words. Were they surprised or did they already suspect he viewed them as his friends by his actions and the intimacies that he had shared with them? I think it was both. I am reminded of Peter struggling to let Jesus wash his feet. Or what about the time Jesus went to the mountaintop taking Peter, James, and John to meet with Elijah and Moses? Jesus had shared some very surprising and intimate things with his disciples. He treated them as friends.

Have you thought about what it means to be friends with Jesus? I grew up singing the hymn by Schiven "What a Friend We Have in Jesus." Have I let the meaning of those words sink deep into my heart? I think it is time for you and me truly to understand what it means to have a friendship with Jesus.

OPENING QUESTIONS

What does the word "friendship" mean to you?

Do you find making and keeping friends easy or hard? Why or why not?

Have you ever considered Jesus your friend?

MEDITATION EXERCISE

For this week, let's use *meditatio scripturarum* to focus on the story of Lazarus's death found in John 11. Place yourself in the text by being one of the characters in the story. What do you learn as you imagine yourself as Mary, Martha, or Lazarus? What is God speaking about to you? As you change characters, how does this change your perspective? What new things do you learn?

PLAYLIST

"Hello Lord"

Conversation Sara Groves

"You Never Let Us Down"

In That Day: Praise Band 10 Maranatha! Praise Band

"Nothing Without You"

Try Bebo Norman

Jesus, Friendship between Equals

KEY READING

In those days Caesar Augustus issued a decree that a census should be taken of the entire Roman world. (This was the first census that took place while Quirinius was governor of Syria.) And everyone went to their own town to register.

So Joseph also went up from the town of Nazareth in Galilee to Judea, to Bethlehem the town of David, because he belonged to the house and line of David. He went there to register with Mary, who was pledged to be married to him and was expecting a child. While they were there, the time came for the baby to be born, and she gave birth to her firstborn, a son. She wrapped him in cloths and placed him in a manger, because there was no guest room available for them.

Luke 2:1–7

We have a fascination with unequal relationships. I think of *Beauty and the Beast* and *The Prince and the Pauper*, stories about two people who came from different walks of life and ended up in an unlikely friendship. What makes it surprising is their lack of equality: rich and poor, beautiful and ugly. Have you noticed that as intriguing as these unbalanced or unequal relationships are, they don't last? The lack of balance eventually brings envy, shame, and even hatred. It is the relationship between equals that seems to last and weather life's storms better.

As I have counseled individuals during the past twenty years, I have met many wonderful people. At times I have found a shared interest or a similar sense of humor. I know that these individuals would make good friends, but as their therapist, I cannot pursue that type of relationship. In the treatment's best interest, I carefully maintain professional boundaries.

So, it is amazing and shocking that God in the form of Jesus would come to offer friendship to you and me. What do we have to offer him? He has all the power in the universe. Angels are available for him to command. Why settle for frail, finite, and sin-riddled humans? Can we survive such a potentially unequal and overwhelming relationship? Remember God had to cover Moses' eyes to protect him from the power of God's glory as God walked by (Exodus 33:18–22)? How can we survive this?

Jesus does not come in "god-form." He comes as a human, as a little baby in a manger. Paul tells us that Jesus did not seek or grasp equality with God, but comes in the form of a servant (Philippians 2:6–7, author's paraphrase). He comes poor with no place to lay his head at night. He is often dependent on others' mercy for food and a place to sleep. He comes in a form that is approachable and sometimes even vulnerable. It is from this place that Jesus reaches out his hand and calls us friend. And it is from this place that we can reach back and accept. How amazing!

❦ Have you known relationships of inequality? How well did they endure?

❦ Do you think your relationship as a friend of Jesus is one of equality or inequality? Why or why not?

❦ What is your reaction as you see the effort Jesus went to in order to relate to you as an equal?

PRAYER

Dear Jesus, thank you for being my friend. You bring everything to this relationship. Help me to see what I bring to you. Equip me to be faithful, loyal, and trustworthy to you as much as you have been to me. Enable me to be a better friend to those around me.

OPTIONAL READINGS

Amos 3:3

John 15:13–17

Jesus, A Friendship of Safety

KEY READING

From that time on Jesus began to explain to his disciples that he must go to Jerusalem and suffer many things at the hands of the elders, the chief priests and the teachers of the law, and that he must be killed and on the third day be raised to life.

Peter took him aside and began to rebuke him. "Never, Lord!" he said. "This shall never happen to you!"

Jesus turned and said to Peter, "Get behind me, Satan! You are a stumbling block to me; you do not have in mind the concerns of God, but merely human concerns."

After six days Jesus took with him Peter, James and John the brother of James, and led them up a high mountain by themselves. There he was transfigured before them. His face shone like the sun, and his clothes became as white as the light. Just then there appeared before them Moses and Elijah, talking with Jesus.

Matthew 16:21–23; 17:1–3

I think the mark of a significant relationship is the degree to which you have permission to be yourself when you are with that person. How much of your deepest feelings or greatest fears do you show to your friend? Someone once told me that a friend of hers called when she was in a dark mood. This friend hung up quickly saying that she would call back when the depressed friend was in a better emotional space. How well do you stand by your friends when they are in pain or in trouble? Do you allow your friends to be themselves in any and all circumstances?

Jesus stands by his friends no matter what the circumstances. I am particularly struck by his relationship with Peter. Have you noticed what an impulsive guy Peter was? He jumped into any situation with both feet. But did this push Jesus away or turn him off? After Jesus shared about the upcoming crucifixion, Peter blurted out that Jesus wasn't going to die. Jesus reprimanded Peter for his denial, then in the very next chapter we see Jesus sharing a powerful, yet intimate moment with Peter. He took him along with James and John up to the mountaintop and was transfigured in front of him while meeting with "the already dead" Moses and Elijah. This doesn't seem like someone who was upset with a friend. If someone damaged my trust, I would be very careful about what I shared with him or her in the future. I'd take fewer risks with that individual. Yet, Jesus didn't constrain himself while with Peter, despite Peter's inappropriate behavior.

There is this same type of safety in Jesus' relationship with Mary and Martha. Their brother was dying, and they pleaded for him to come. He arrived four days after Lazarus' death. Both sisters went to meet Jesus alone and both had angry, pleading words for him: "If you had been here my brother would not have died" (John 11:21, 32). Jesus wasn't offended by their hurtful, accusing words. In fact, he was moved by them and wept. We can have this same level of safety and honesty with Jesus. We can be ourselves, whether silly, impulsive, ignorant, fearful, or angry. Jesus won't be put off by us or feel ashamed of us. He will understand and be moved.

❦ Can you think of other examples of Jesus encouraging and allowing others to be themselves?

❦ In the past, how safe have you felt with Jesus?

❦ What part of yourself have you been hesitant to share with Jesus? Why?

PRAYER

Dear Jesus, thank you for being my friend. You allow me to be myself. I don't have this privilege in many places in my life and find this level of transparency hard to maintain, even with you. Please forgive me for this fear. Strengthen my trust in you so I can share all parts of myself with you.

OPTIONAL READINGS

Matthew 14:25–32

John 11:1–6, 17–44

Jesus, Friendship of Reciprocity

KEY READING

They went to a place called Gethsemane, and Jesus said to his disciples, "Sit here while I pray." He took Peter, James and John along with him, and he began to be deeply distressed and troubled. "My soul is overwhelmed with sorrow to the point of death," he said to them. "Stay here and keep watch."

Then he returned to his disciples and found them sleeping. "Simon," he said to Peter, "are you asleep? Couldn't you keep watch for one hour? Watch and pray so that you will not fall into temptation. The spirit is willing, but the flesh is weak."

Once more he went away and prayed the same thing. When he came back, he again found them sleeping, because their eyes were heavy. They did not know what to say to him.

Mark 14:32–34, 37–4(

Another important characteristic of great friendships is reciprocity Good friends mutually need each other. Both members in the relationship store up ideas and stories to tell one another. They each look forward to the time they will have together, and they independently make efforts to arrange such times. Relationships without some level o reciprocity or mutuality don't last for very long. Reciprocity suggests a degree of dependence. One does not look forward to another person's presence unless one needs him or her, unless in some way he or she helps to make another's life more complete.

It seems almost silly that I would bring up this characteristic in terms of Jesus' relationship with any of us. How can Jesus, the Son of God, need you or me? He is complete in himself. He is part of the Trinity (Father, Son, and Spirit). How could a relationship with one of us bring any more wholeness or satisfaction to his life? Surprisingly, Scriptures point to his desire for a relationship with us.

Jesus says, "Here I am! I stand at the door and knock. If anyone hears my voice and opens the door, I will come in and eat with him, and he with me" (Revelation 3:20). The mutuality alluded to in this verse is intriguing. Jesus doesn't come in to feed me, but to eat with me. I have something Jesus' longs for.

Jesus' desire for intimacy also shows up in the mountaintop and Garden of Gethsemane stories. Jesus brings his closest disciples to share in some of the most important and painful moments of his life. Why does Jesus take the disciples with him? I think part of the reason for this decision is because he longs not only to hear yours and my secrets, but also to tell us the secrets of his heart. Also, could it be that a part of what he looks for is support? I think I must be very careful with this point. Jesus only does what the Father, God, tells him to do—he doesn't need our approval. But Jesus does share exciting and difficult moments, not just as object lessons, but as something more. Does he still do that with you and me? It seems so.

- Have you ever thought that Jesus might want to tell you secrets of his heart?

- Can you think of a time when you felt Jesus shared something personal with you?

- How does knowing that Jesus wants a reciprocal relationship change your perspective?

PRAYER

Dear Jesus, thank you for being my friend. I am shocked that you want a re ciprocal relationship with me. I am not sure I have anything to share with you Show me what you desire from me. Help me to become a friend who listens to your secrets.

OPTIONAL READINGS

Matthew 17:1–9

Colossians 2:2–4

Jesus, a Friend Who Lays Down His Life

KEY READING

"As the Father has loved me, so have I loved you. Now remain in my love. If you keep my commands, you will remain in my love, just as I have kept my Father's commands and remain in his love. I have told you this so that my joy may be in you and that your joy may be complete. My command is this: Love each other as I have loved you. Greater love has no one than this: to lay down one's life for one's friends. You are my friends if you do what I command. I no longer call you servants, because a servant does not know his master's business. Instead, I have called you friends, for everything that I learned from my Father I have made known to you."

John 15:9–15

Have you ever had a party and invited your closest friend? The kind of friend who causes the party to start when he or she enters the room? Didn't you feel grateful that this individual cared enough about you to make the effort to be at your party? In fact, you knew this person was a true friend because nothing would have gotten in the way of him or her attending your event.

I believe the most important quality of a deep friendship is self-sacrifice. True friends put each other first. True friends come through for each other.

Jesus understands what it means to be this kind of friend. He doesn't just show up at your birthday party or when you are sick. He is there whenever you need him, whether you are happy, sad, disappointed, or angry. He knows very well what it means to be a true friend. He holds nothing back, not even himself. Jesus so desires a friendship with you that he gave up his own life in order for this relationship to occur.

Unfortunately, this kind of friendship is rare. Most of us know the pain that comes from others not coming through for us. Jesus understands this and promises never to hurt us in this way. In fact, he knows this kind of pain first hand. Judas, after spending three years listening, sharing meals and learning from Jesus, betrayed him for thirty pieces of silver (Matthew 26:14–16). I cannot imagine how this must have hurt Jesus. If only this was the worst of it. Jesus' closest disciples couldn't stay awake to pray with him after he told them he was troubled to the point of death (Mark 14:32–41) Three times Peter denied knowing Jesus (Luke 22:54–62) and most of the disciples scattered as Jesus was being tortured and crucified.

Jesus understands betrayal and promises not to betray you or me. The very last words of Jesus found in Matthew 28 are promises never to leave us. He said, "And surely I am with you always, to the very end of the age (Matthew 28:20b). We have never known a friend like Jesus. He is the greatest kind of friend.

❦ What kind of friendships have you had?

❦ Tell of a time when friend came through for you in such a way that it left you deeply touched.

❦ Have you thought of Jesus as your truest friend? How does it change your relationship with him to think of him this way?

PRAYER

Dear Jesus, thank you for being my friend. You are my truest friend. I am completely shocked, moved, and touched that you withhold nothing from me, not even your own life. I have never known anyone to love me so much. Thank you for your sacrifice and friendship.

OPTIONAL READINGS

Romans 5:6–8

Concluding Thoughts

Once I was contacted by a prospective client. Her previous therapy had ended and she was looking for a new counselor. After obtaining my name as a possible option, she called with a few questions about my treatment style. She wanted to know if I would be open to going out to lunch with her periodically. She wondered about this because her last therapist regularly went out to lunch with her. This alarmed me since this practice was unethical and might have compromised the effectiveness of her previous treatment experience. I explained I wouldn't be having lunch and why I believed it wouldn't be beneficial to treatment. She hung up disappointed and without making an appointment. I knew that I could not be both her friend and therapist if treatment was to be productive.

Jesus does not have this same limitation. He is able to be our friend and our healer. We wholeheartedly can embrace friendship with Jesus. And, in this wonderful companion-ship, we will discover deep understanding, constant support, and never-ending security. Jesus, after all, is the perfect Friend.

Chapter 5

The Returning King

KEY SCRIPTURE

"The kingdom of the world has become the kingdom of our Lord and of his Christ, and he will reign for ever and ever."

Revelation 11:15

A common counseling theme is the desire and search for justice. Betrayal and abuse occur too frequently. Clients struggle with the unfairness of life. Where were their parents or God when they were being emotionally or physically hurt? How can they forgive their perpetrator when this individual often goes unpunished?

All of us have been wronged at some point in time. Unfortunately, life rarely deals with these injustices in a fair and equitable manner. The legal system may penalize criminals, but it usually does not heal the wound left by the victimization. Often we are left hurt and angry. We need a government that can bring real fairness and peace to our hurting hearts.

Has such a government ever existed? When Israel became a nation, it needed some form of rulership. Originally, God planned this nation to be his own (Leviticus 20:26). However, Israel sought to be like other nations and have a king (1 Samuel 8:7). God granted its desires. He first selected Saul and then David from among the common folks. Israel's godly kings brought prosperity, whereas its godless kings brought moral decay, idolatry, and hardship. How would history have been different if God had been the king of Israel?

The human heart has a deep longing to live in a utopian society; a place where real justice and peace exists. Jesus comprehended such longings. He told the crowd that those who desire righteousness would be satisfied (Matthew 5:6). He understood the desire for justice. In fact, he told his listeners that individuals who hunger for this kind of peace were blessed. Blessed? How were they blessed? Those hearing his word went home to the same situation they had left earlier that day. Jesus was revealing that one day he would come again and make all things right.

So, God's original plan for rulership was not lost. Jesus is our returning King. He is ushering in God's kingdom. This is a different kind of kingship, one that has no end. It will be ruled by someone who is human, like us, and has lived among us, but who is also fully divine and without sin. When Jesus returns as our King, he will set up a government that will bring a real and abiding peace.

Where is this kingdom and how does one enter it borders? When you and I accept Jesus' gift of salvation, we move from the dominion of sin into the rulership and authority of Jesus. Someday, all will acknowledge this authority when every knee will bow and proclaim Jesus as King (Philippians 2:9-11, author's paraphrase). In this new and coming kingdom, we will experience a community life that lives rightly with God.

OPENING QUESTIONS

What comes to your mind when you think of the word "King?"

HEALING WITHOUT LIMITS

How do you think life would be different under a monarchy versus a democracy?

MEDITATION EXERCISE

I would like to return to the practice of breath prayer. Remember this is a short, simple prayer that can be said in one breath. For the purpose of this chapter, I suggest you use a sentence that focuses on Jesus' identity as king, such as "Jesus is the King of kings" or "King Jesus, reign in my life." Find a quiet place where you can be alone and take five to fifteen minutes to focus on your breath prayer. This prayer is to be silently spoken within yourself in a relaxed manner. How is God using this prayer to speak to you? What is your reaction to the words? How are you responding to God? After several minutes of repeating the breath prayer, reflect on what you are hearing from God. You may want to add those reflections to your journal.

PLAYLIST

"You Reign"

All That Is Within Me MercyMe

"Here Is Our King"

A Collision David Crowder Band

"The Lord's Prayer (Deliver Us)"

You Deliver Me Selah

"Hold Me Jesus"

Every Time I Breathe Big Daddy Weave

Jesus, A Different Kind of King, Part 1

KEY READING

He grew up before him like a tender shoot,
and like a root out of dry ground.
He had no beauty or majesty to attract us to him,
nothing in his appearance that we should desire him.
He was despised and rejected by mankind,
a man of suffering, and familiar with pain.
Like one from whom people hide their faces
he was despised, and we held him in low esteem.
He was oppressed and afflicted,
yet he did not open his mouth;
he was led like a lamb to the slaughter,
and as a sheep before its shearers is silent,
so he did not open his mouth.

Isaiah 53:2–3, 7

Israel's first king was Saul, a handsome man. He was a very flawed king, despite being a strong military leader. He helped to unify Israel in a time when the country was vulnerable to invasion by outside tribes and powers. Saul initially was reluctant about being king. Samuel anointed Saul as the one chosen by God to lead the Israelites. Later, when questioned about his experiences with Samuel, Saul neglected to reveal the most important detail: his anointing! When Samuel pointed him out as God's choice for king, Saul hid himself from view. What was going on? I would have been worried about these traits if I saw them in my president-elect. Does he really want to be king? What kind of ruler will he be if he is that ambivalent about his selection?

Jesus is a different kind of king. He does not have the outward characteristics that say he would make a good king. In fact, Isaiah tells us there is "nothing in his appearance that we should desire him" (Isaiah 53:2). But he is not a reluctant leader. Jesus willingly obeys God. He does not hide himself from his mission and destiny. He faces it head on. Jesus tells his disciples that "my food is to do the will of him who sent me and to finish his work" (John 4:34). We can be confident of Jesus' acceptance of his role as king. He takes this mantle squarely upon his shoulders. There are no half-hearted efforts with him. Jesus is not an ambivalent king.

✻ Have you seen a political candidate's appearance affect public opinion? How did it change the election outcome?

✻ Do you find outward characteristics influence your decision in choosing a president?

✻ Isaiah tells us there is nothing attractive or majestic about Jesus, yet he is our King. What is your reaction to this description?

PRAYER

Dear Jesus, thank you for being my willing King. It gives me confidence knowing that you approach this role with your whole heart. Teach me what it means to have you reign over me and my life.

OPTIONAL READINGS

1 Samuel 9:1–2, 15–17; 10:1–24

Luke 22:42

John 12:27–28

Jesus, A Different Kind of King, Part 2

KEY READING

Who, being in very nature God,
did not consider equality with God something to be used to his own
advantage;
rather, he made himself nothing
by taking the very nature[b] of a servant,
being made in human likeness.
And being found in appearance as a man,
he humbled himself
by becoming obedient to death—
even death on a cross!

Philippians 2:6–8

Have you ever given instructions to someone, only to find out he didn't follow the directions and then justified his actions? Saul was that kind of king. He was disobedient to the will of God and refused to take responsibility for the mess he made. I've worked with a few of these people. I find I cannot trust them. They are frustrating since they often impede long-range goals. As team members, they are unpredictable since they have their own best interest at heart. I wonder what Israel could have accomplished under King Saul's rule if he had been a different kind of king.

Jesus is not disobedient and arrogant; he is an obedient and humble King. Repeatedly, we see him following God's directions regardless of the personal cost. He faces rejection, enemies trying to kill him, misunderstanding, and even betrayal and abandonment by his disciples, yet he never wavers from God's will. When faced with accusations, Jesus doesn't justify himself and blame others. He quietly humbles himself Jesus never retaliates or threatens to get even (1 Peter 2:23). He is the King of the universe with all things at his command: angels, nature, even people; yet, he never attempts to get even with those who hurt him.

Jesus is an amazing person. He is someone we can trust. He doesn't justify, get even, or shirk responsibilities. He is someone we can follow anywhere because he will always keep the objective in mind while taking responsibility for the outcome. What an awesome king he makes. Jesus truly is a different kind of King.

❋ When you think of kings or queens, who comes to your mind? What kind of ruler was this individual?

❋ What characteristics do you think make for a good ruler?

❋ What is your reaction to qualities that Jesus possesses as king: obedient and humble?

❋ How do these qualities strengthen him as king?

HEALING WITHOUT LIMITS

PRAYER

Dear Jesus, thank you for being an obedient and humble King. We have seen the disaster that happens under the rulership of kings who are weak and arrogant. Help me to submit to your authority and to strengthen my trust in you.

OPTIONAL READINGS

1 Samuel 13:8–14, 15:2–3, 9, 20–30

Isaiah 53:7

John 12:27–28

Living in Jesus' Kingdom

KEY READING

"He will wipe every tear from their eyes. There will be no more death or mourning or crying or pain, for the old order of things has passed away."

He who was seated on the throne said, "I am making everything new!" Then he said, "Write this down, for these words are trustworthy and true."

He said to me: "It is done. I am the Alpha and the Omega, the Beginning and the End. To the thirsty I will give water without cost from the spring of the water of life."

Revelation 21:4–6

The descriptions of the new heaven and new earth found in Revelation 20–22 are fantastic. What will it be like to walk on streets of gold? To have God be my light? To live with no more death, disease, sin, or darkness? All of this will be fantastic, but it doesn't just end with a perfect environment and perfect body. I will be living in a realm that will be perfectly governed.

What would it be like to live in such a world? As I listen to people's stories during individual counseling sessions, I hear of great injustice and unfairness. Some people don't get what should be coming to them and others seem luckier than they deserve. Jesus promises to rule with justice and righteousness. There will be real equality and true justice. He also promises real, lasting peace. It won't be like the kind of truces we see in the Middle East, where there are no real compromises and hostility still seethes underneath the cease-fires. No, this will be a place where everyone lives harmoniously with God, with ourselves, and with each other. It will be a government that cannot be upset or overthrown. I can hardly fathom such a place.

This also will be a kingdom where God and Jesus are readily available. How many times do I pray only to feel like my prayers are stuck in my throat? I struggle with my doubt that God hears my pleadings. What would it be like to live where God is accessible, where I can know without a shadow of a doubt that my concerns, needs, and even musings are important and heard by God? I believe that Jesus' kingdom will be such a place. We will have a more personal experience of God. I can't wait.

- What do you think of when you imagine living on the new earth?

- Which descriptions found in Revelation 20–22 excite you the most? Why?

- What do you think it will be like to have a more accessible relationship with God?

PRAYER

Dear Jesus, your kingdom sounds wonderful. Magnify the hope and wonder in me so I might live for your kingdom, not for worldly pleasures.

OPTIONAL READINGS

Hebrews 12:28

Revelation 21:15, 21 & 27, 22:3–5

Jesus' Kingdom in Me

KEY READING

Once, on being asked by the Pharisees when the kingdom of God would come, Jesus replied, "The coming of the kingdom of God is not something that can be observed, nor will people say, 'Here it is,' or 'There it is,' because the kingdom of God is in your midst."

Luke 17:20–21

The strange part of Jesus' kingdom is that it is not just something we are waiting to enter upon death, it has also come now. I have heard it explained as "here, but not yet." What does that mean? John the Baptist told the crowds that the kingdom of heaven was near (Matthew 3:2); yet, Jesus announced that the kingdom of heaven was here within you. Huh? How confusing! What changed?

Jesus is the change. Because of his birth, death, and resurrection, God now lives in our hearts. We can enter into God's presence through Jesus. Because of this change we are literally being born into the kingdom of heaven despite still being here in this sin-filled world (John 3:3–6).

The kingdom of heaven can break into this desperate world through each of us. What does this mean? When we are followers of Jesus, his realm is established in our hearts. We can increase his rule by our submission to his will. When we forgive someone who has hurt us, the forgiven person experiences a taste of the kingdom of heaven. For example, if we practice patience in the grocery line with the new cashier, that individual experiences God's love and grace. We can be the vehicle by which the world experiences Jesus' kingdom.

I have experienced the Holy Spirit working through me in counseling situations. Exactly the right words or insights will come to me. Through my obedience to God's will, my clients experience a taste of the kingdom of heaven. Someday Jesus will come back and usher in his kingdom in its fullness, but for right now, he brings it through you and me. That is an exciting, yet sobering thought.

❧ Your obedient actions may be the means by which others experience Jesus' kingdom. What is your reaction to this idea?

❧ Does knowing this change anything for you? If so, what and how?

❧ Write about one recent experience you have had where God used you to touch someone else.

PRAYER

Dear Jesus, thank you for bringing your kingdom to my heart. I want your reign to increase in my life. Let your love for the world shine brighter in my life.

OPTIONAL READINGS

Matthew 13:1–9, 18–22

Mark 4:26–29

Concluding Thoughts

During the course of treatment, one of my clients had a family member murdered. I remember the appointment after this tragic event. This person was devastated by the loss and very angry. There was an overwhelming desire for the perpetrator to be found and brought to justice. The murder crushed the family and left a gaping hole that could never be filled. The dead could not be restored to the family on this side of eternity. No court system could bring wholeness to the family. I, as the therapist, yearned for justice.

Jesus is returning once again. This time he will come as our King and bring lasting peace and real justice. He will bring a kingdom that will never end. Our desire for righteousness is not in vain. He will make all the wrongs right once again. But this kingdom can start now in us. When we practice love, forgiveness, and kindness, God's grace is revealed to the world. While we wait for the returning King, we will be his conduit to bring his justice and peace to this desperate world.

Chapter 6

Our Bridegroom

KEY SCRIPTURE

"Let us rejoice and be glad and give him glory! For the wedding of the Lamb has come, and his bride has made herself ready."

Revelation 19:7

Recently I went to a romantic movie. The theater was packed with women and teenage girls. I heard the audience laugh and sigh as we watched the developing love. I came out of the experience with an incredible longing. It was an actual physical ache in my chest that lasted for several hours for such an intimate connection with another; for such desire and attraction. There was a scene when the heroine told the strong, virile, handsome suitor, "I trust you." Despite his strength and dangerousness, he was trustworthy to her. Oh, to feel such love and safety. This reminds me of the scene between Jesus and his disciples. He was preparing them for the upcoming trials he would be facing with his crucifixion and death looming. He told them, "Do not let your hearts be troubled . . . trust also in me" (John 14:1). What if we substituted these words in a love scene between the knight in shining armor and his princess? Can you see Jesus comforting his future bride with these words as he prepares to slay the dragon?

Throughout the years, as I've counseled many people, I have found this same longing in most women. What is it about the female gender that thirsts for such intimacy? We seek out and soak up stories of true love, like *Cinderella*, *Sleeping Beauty*, and *Beauty and the Beast*. I remember thinking that my marriage would capture this kind of love, only to find out like many other women that it somehow misses the mark. Don't get me wrong, marriage is great. I love the marital intimacy, the camaraderie, and the companionship, but it doesn't have some "essence" that these fairy tales describe. What is "this thing" that women pursue? Is it real? Should it be pursued? Is it God-ordained?

God's word assures me that the female longing is God-given. Reading Solomon's Song of Songs makes me blush because I see the same intensity and passion I watched in that recent romantic film. I am not used to thinking of this passion as spiritual, but I believe there is something very profound about the longing I felt during the movie. I think it is this same hunger that Madame Guyon was describing when she wrote, "I slept not all night because Thy love, O my God, flowed in me like delicious oil, and burned as a fire. . . I love God far more than the most affectionate lover among men loves his earthly attachment."[4] Jesus tells us that he is our Bridegroom and that we are his Bride. This is shocking, almost uncomfortable imagery. What if it is more than imagery? What if it is literal? What does it mean to me and you? How does it change things for us?

I have come to the conclusion that Jesus is the most radical of lovers. The whole Bible is a love letter written to you and me about his desire for us. We catch glimpses of Jesus' passion in some of our fairy tales, but his love is even more beautiful and perfect. The psalmist understood this when he wrote, "As the deer pants for streams of water, so my soul pants for you, O God" (Psalm 42:1).

OPENING QUESTIONS

What is your reaction to the idea of Jesus as your Bridegroom?

What comes to your mind when you think of Jesus this way?

MEDITATION EXERCISE

Choose one of the songs in the playlist below to focus on during your meditation time. You may have one of your own songs you would prefer to use. I encourage you to choose a song that is worshipful and focuses on Jesus. As you listen, imagine Jesus being right next to you. Let yourself experience your love for him and his love for you. You might want to jot down your reaction and thoughts after the song finishes.

"How He Loves"

Church Music David Crowder Band

"Revelation Song"

Fearless Phillips, Craig & Dean

"Jesus, You're Beautiful"

All Right Here Sara Groves

"Love You More"

In That Day: Praise Band 10 Maranatha! Praise Band

Jesus and Vows of Commitment

KEY READING

"I am the Lord your God, who brought you out of Egypt, out of the land of slavery."

"You shall have no other gods before me."

"You shall not make for yourself an image in the form of anything in heaven above or on the earth beneath or in the waters below. You shall not bow down to them or worship them; for I, the Lord your God, am a jealous God, punishing the children for the sin of the parents to the third and fourth generation of those who hate me, but showing love to a thousand generations of those who love me and keep my commandments."

"You shall not misuse the name of the Lord your God, for the Lord will not hold anyone guiltless who misuses his name."

Hear, O Israel: The Lord our God, the Lord is one. Love the Lord your God with all your heart and with all your soul and with all your strength. These commandments that I give you today are to be on your hearts.

Deuteronomy 5:6–12, 6:4–6

Some of my best spiritual times occur during my walks. I usually listen to worship music to pass the exercise time with praise and prayer. Recently, I was listening to the song "No Other" by Susan Ashton, Margaret Becker, and Christine Dente. I heard words of promises that God would be my all.

I was stunned as I listened. I suddenly thought of the first four laws of the Ten Commandments (Deuteronomy 5:6–12). Aren't they all commitments or promises of exclusivity similar to what we make in our marriage vows? Aren't we saying to God that he is our one and only love, he will be the center of our hearts and lives, and there will be no other? I had never considered these commandments as love promises.

Have you ever secretly loved someone who didn't realize your attraction or feel the same interest? Everything that person does that might suggest fondness toward you, fills your heart with excitement and hope. Everything he or she does that neglects or ignores you, fills you with pain and disappointment. What if Jesus feels that same way for you and me? What if he is waiting for you to see his love for you and to turn to him? Jesus longs to be the center of your life; not just for your submission to his will, but for your love and fidelity. He wants the same devotion that any lover longs to have: to be the one and only in the heart of his beloved.

✤ What is your reaction to the perspective of the first four commandments possibly being love promises?

✤ Have you ever thought of Jesus longing for your attention and interest in him as a lover waiting for the affection of his beloved?

✤ What is your reaction to this? Why?

PRAYER

Dear Jesus, thinking of you as my bridegroom is new and strange. Increase in me an awareness of your great love for me. Help me to become more aware of your delight in me as your beloved.

OPTIONAL READINGS

Zephaniah 3:17

Matthew 22:36–38

John 15:9–11

The Marriage Proposal and Bride Price

KEY READING

And he took bread, gave thanks and broke it, and gave it to them, saying, "This is my body given for you; do this in remembrance of me."

In the same way, after the supper he took the cup, saying, "This cup is the new covenant in my blood, which is poured out for you. But the hand of him who is going to betray me is with mine on the table. The Son of Man will go as it has been decreed. But woe to that man who betrays him!" They began to question among themselves which of them it might be who would do this.

Luke 22:19–23

The Jewish tradition of marriage is very different from our own. I will take the next two days to focus on this and how it parallels Jesus' relationship with his bride, the church.

The first step in the Jewish marriage process is the betrothal. It is a contract between the man and the woman. The prospective bridegroom's father meets with the father of the bride to establish the dowry or bride-price.

Imagine God establishing a dowry for the church. It cost Jesus his life, which he willingly gave. The author of Hebrews tells us Jesus considered this sacrifice a "joy" (Hebrews 12:2). Can you imagine his excitement at the prospect of marriage to his adored beloved? His Father tells him her bride-price, which he jumps at since it means his heart's desire will soon be his.

In the Jewish tradition of Jesus' day, the couple sealed the marriage contract with a symbol of the covenant made between the two young lovers. The bridegroom fills a cup of wine and passes it to his bride to be. He tells her that the wine represents the new covenant they are making to each other.

Imagine Jesus looking at his new bride, the church, as he passes her the cup of wine at the communion table. We drink of this cup, accepting his marriage proposal and become his purchased bride.

Despite the fact that the wedding has not occurred, the Jewish bride commits herself to her husband. She is his alone. She is set apart from all others and will keep herself pure to honor the commitment and covenant between herself and her bridegroom.

Just like the Jewish bride, you and I are set apart or "sanctified." We belong to no other. We are his precious one. Can you imagine how painful it must be to Jesus when we break this vow by moving other concerns, relationships, or pursuits into the center of our lives? Just as he faithfully commits himself to us, he longs for our faithfulness to him.

❋ What is your reaction to the parallels between the Jewish marriage proposal and Jesus' covenant with us?

❋ What part is the most significant to you? Why?

❋ What part do you struggle with? Why?

PRAYER

Dear Jesus, thank you for paying my bride-price with your life. Your love is overwhelming. I am not as faithful as I should be to you. Forgive me and help me to make you the center of my life.

OPTIONAL READINGS

1 Corinthians 6:19–20

Ephesians 5:25–27

The Wedding

KEY READING

"At that time the kingdom of heaven will be like ten virgins who took their lamps and went out to meet the bridegroom. Five of them were foolish and five were wise. The foolish ones took their lamps but did not take any oil with them. The wise ones, however, took oil in jars along with their lamps. The bridegroom was a long time in coming, and they all became drowsy and fell asleep.

At midnight the cry rang out: 'Here's the bridegroom! Come out to meet him!'

Then all the virgins woke up and trimmed their lamps. The foolish ones said to the wise, 'Give us some of your oil; our lamps are going out.'

'No,' they replied, 'there may not be enough for both us and you. Instead, go to those who sell oil and buy some for yourselves.'

But while they were on their way to buy the oil, the bridegroom arrived. The virgins who were ready went in with him to the wedding banquet. And the door was shut.

Later the others also came. 'Lord, Lord,' they said, 'open the door for us!'

But he replied, 'Truly I tell you, I don't know you.'

Therefore keep watch, because you do not know the day or the hour."

Matthew 25:1–13

Next, we see our eager bridegroom at his father's home. He leaves the side of his bride in order to prepare a place for her. He goes home and begins to work on an addition to his father's house. This will be their own residence, designed and built by his hands. His father oversees the project, only giving the nod of approval when the new home is fit for a for a queen. This building project may take anywhere from six to twelve months. The exact day is unknown.

The bride waits, knowing on any given day she may hear the shofar blow announcing the arrival of her bridegroom. Night after night she listens at her window, wondering if this will be the night when her husband comes to get her for the wedding. One evening she hears the long awaited call of the shofar, and she dresses as a queen to meet her king (Psalm 45:14–15; Isaiah 61:10; Ezekiel 16:11–13). With great excitement, the streets are lit up by lamps, lighting the groom's way to her house. He reaches his bride and escorts her to the waiting wedding feast where guests have already assembled. There the party begins.

What a romantic story, yet Jesus tells us this is to be our future. Just as the bride waits to hear the shofar announcing the arrival of her groom, so, too, we wait to hear the trumpet announcing Jesus' second coming. The covenant has been made, the dowry paid; will you and I be found faithful and waiting with our lamps trimmed and full of oil? Or asleep and unprepared? Jesus, as we speak, is preparing a perfect place for us. God is making sure that no detail is missed; that it is just right for us. We are to stay alert, keep our hearts pure, and watch for his return. Are we ready?

✻ What stood out to you as you read the wedding tradition? Why?

✻ Does it seem real that you are Jesus' beloved? Why or why not?

✻ How prepared are you for Jesus' return? What more do you need to do?

HEALING WITHOUT LIMITS

PRAYER

Jesus, sometimes I don't believe that I am your beloved—that your relationship with me is personal. Please expand an awareness in my heart of your deep, abiding, personal love for me. Help me to be alert, with my heart ready for your return.

OPTIONAL READINGS

John 14:1–4

1 Corinthians 15:50–54

Being the Bride of Jesus

KEY READING

"Now, brothers and sisters, about times and dates we do not need to write to you, for you know very well that the day of the Lord will come like a thief in the night. While people are saying, "Peace and safety," destruction will come on them suddenly, as labor pains on a pregnant woman, and they will not escape.

But you, brothers and sisters, are not in darkness so that this day should surprise you like a thief. You are all children of the light and children of the day. We do not belong to the night or to the darkness. So then, let us not be like others, who are asleep, but let us be awake and sober.

Rejoice always, pray continually, give thanks in all circumstances; for this is God's will for you in Christ Jesus."

1 Thessalonians 5:1–6, 16–18

You and I are in a difficult period of our life with Jesus. He is here, but not fully yet. I like the word "shadowland" to explain this place. This word captures what life often feels like for me. There are too many times and places in my life that are filled with pain, fear, and suffering; yet, I have glimpses of something more, something so beautiful and perfect that I ache for it. Someday this longing will be met. Someday Jesus will come for me and bring me home. Then I will finally and truly "want for nothing" (Psalm 23:1, author's paraphrase).

But for now, I live here, in this sin-filled, imperfect place. What does it mean to be the bride of Jesus today? How should this affect what I do? Two things come to my mind: I am to love Jesus and grow closer to him; and I am to love the people around me so they will be drawn to Jesus

(Matthew 22:36–40). There have been many sermons on these two great commandments. I know it strengthens my relationship with Jesus to have a regular prayer life and to read his word. I also know I am to show kindness, patience, and love to those around me. Have I considered what this means, besides being a religious practice?

My spiritual practices are much more. They are like love letters and midnight strolls with Jesus. When I pray or spend time in the Bible, I am talking to the lover of my heart. When I love the world around me, like my cranky neighbor, the shut-in down the street, or the harried cashier, I love Jesus by loving his hoped for bride-to-be since every person in the world is either Jesus' bride (by his or her personal commitment to him) or his longed for bride-to-be. His bride-to-be is comprised of individuals who are not in a personal relationship with Jesus either because they don't know him, or they haven't recognized their inner longings as a desire for Jesus. Yet, he deeply loves and longs for each of them. My kindness to the world around me recognizes each person's value to Jesus. It becomes a conduit of Jesus, reaching out to those who don't know him, drawing all people into a possible relationship with him. I become Jesus' hands and feet so he can touch the world he loves.

I am the bride of Jesus. I can live with hope, peace, and expectancy. This is but a foretaste of what is to come.

🐾 What does it change for you to know you are the bride of Jesus?

🐾 How does being the bride of Jesus affect your daily life?

How does it change your view of the people you encounter to think of them as Jesus' hoped for bride-to-be?

PRAYER

Dear Jesus, I can hardly wait for your return. I desire to be complete. Let this hope and joy make me a more loving person to you and to the world around me.

OPTIONAL READINGS

Revelation 21:1–4; 22:1–5

Concluding Thoughts

An effective counseling relationship should create such a safe, accepting environment that it encourages the client's real self to emerge and to address his unmet emotional needs.[5] But there is a limit to the therapist-client relationship. Their contact only occurs during therapy sessions. Counselors are not to associate with their clients outside of this confine without risking the treatment benefits. Therapists also are human and, therefore, vulnerable to communication errors, misunderstandings, and their personal lives interfering with their professional relationships.

Jesus is more than the ultimate therapist, he is our bridegroom. He perfectly relates to us. He understands our greatest emotional and spiritual needs and promises to meet our deepest longings. This is an exclusive relationship. Just as he promises to fulfill our desire for intimacy with him; we are to be faithfully committed to him. We are to keep ourselves pure and wait for his return. He is to be our sole focus. Jesus is returning again to claim us, his bride.

Conclusion

As I examine all the various roles Jesus occupies in our lives, I am aware how they overlap continuously. He is the priest who presents the offering of the lamb on our behalf. The lamb is himself. He is the tabernacle or the dwelling place of God that the priest enters to deliver the sacrifice. He is the light which opens our eyes to our need for such an offering. On it goes.

We are surrounded on all sides by Christ—all to enable us to enter God's presence. How overwhelming! How inconceivable! It drives home the fact that, above all things, God passionately desires a relationship with us. Look to what extreme, almost ridiculous measures he has gone to achieve such a relationship. Who takes such risks? Yet, the God of the universe puts himself in a vulnerable position. No wonder the angels were amazed as they sung out on the night of Jesus' birth.

"I bring you good news of great joy that will be for all the people. Today in the town of David a Savior has been born to you; he is Christ the Lord. This will be a sign to you: You will find a baby wrapped in cloths and lying in a manger. Suddenly a great company of the heavenly host appeared with the angel, praising God and saying, 'Glory to God in the highest, and on earth peace to men on whom his favor rests.'"

Luke 2:14

They must have marveled to see God in the form of Jesus reaching toward you and me. He is still reaching out to touch and love us today.

Sources

Chapter 2: The Lamb of God

[1]"Lessons by Corrie Ten Boom." *How Shall They Hear Without a Preacher?* *http://www.amazinggracebaptistchurchkjv.com/Download60.html.* (Assessed January 29, 2010).

Chapter 3: Our Kinsman-Redeemer

[2]Edersheim, Alfred. *Sketches of Jewish Social Life.* Peabody, Massachusetts: Hendrickson Publishers, Inc., 1994, 145.

[3]"Kinsman Redeemer." *Hope of Israel Baptist Mission. http://www. hopeofisrael.net/index.php?option=com_content&task=view&id=37&Item id=32.* (Accessed September 21, 2007).

Chapter 6: The Good Shepherd

[4]Winkworth, Susanna. *Life of Madame de lat Mothe Guyon.* London: H.R. Allenson, Limited, 1920.

[5]Winnicott, D.W. The use of an object, *International Journal of Psychoanalysis* 50 (1969), 711-716.

The author welcomes comments. You can find her at www. livinglife2thefullest.com.

Made in the USA
Middletown, DE
27 January 2016